D1360013

Ron and Joyce Cave, both senior officials of the Cambridgeshire Educational Authority, have written and developed these books to be read by children on their own.

A simple question is asked about each topic discussed and is then immediately answered.

A second, more general question follows which is designed to provoke further thinking by the child and may require parental assistance.

The answers to these second questions are found at the end of the book.

Designed and produced by
Aladdin Books Ltd
70 Old Compton Street · London W1
for: The Archon Press Ltd
8 Butter Market · Ipswich

Published in the U.S.A. 1983 by
Gloucester Press
387 Park Avenue South · New York NY 10016

Library of Congress Catalog
Card No: 82-84095

ISBN 531-03471-2

Ron and Joyce Cave

Illustrated by
Roger Phillips and Paul Cooper

GLOUCESTER PRESS
New York · Toronto

Warships

Ever since men first paddled dugout canoes, armed with sticks and stones, ships have been used in battle. The first specially-built warships were made over 2,500 years ago. These were powered either by teams of oarsmen or by sail. It was not until the invention of steam power that warships could become the huge, thickly armored giants that sail in the world's navies today.

"Suffren" class French Destroyer

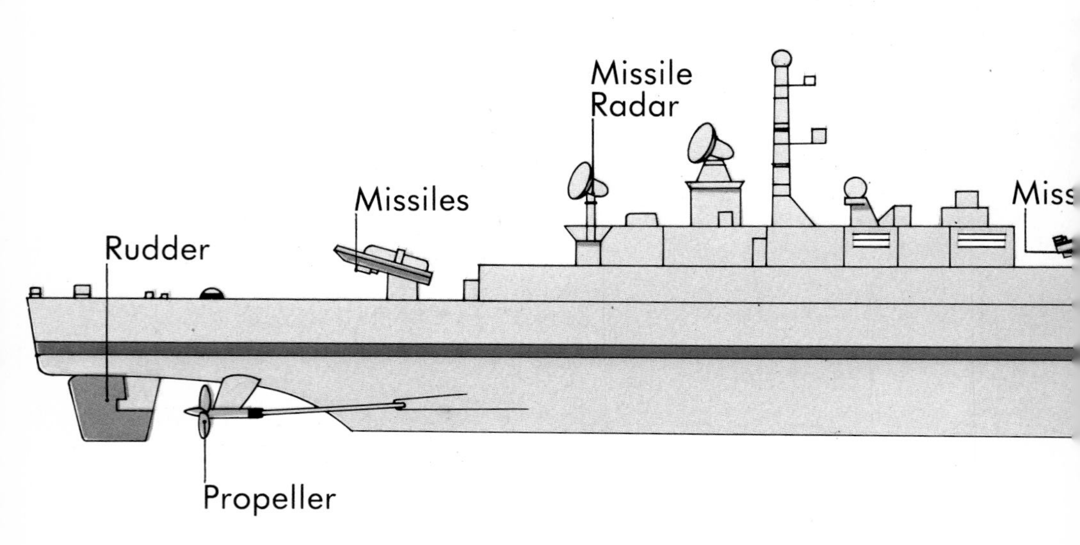

This book will show you some of the famous warships of the past, as well as some of the different types of modern warship. Shown here is a destroyer, armed with powerful missiles and guns. It uses radar and computers, both for navigation and to fire its weapons in attack and defence. Its massive turbine engines can drive it through the water at speeds of more than 30 km/h (19 mph).

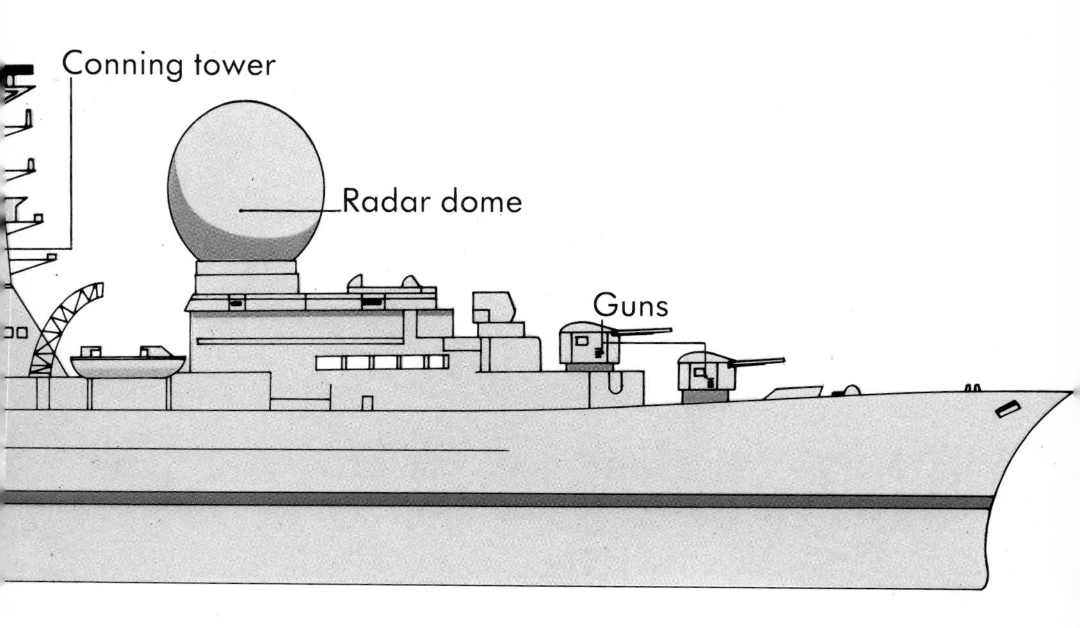

Early warships

The earliest warships had just one set of oarsmen. To increase the ship's power, a second bank was added, and later, a third. Warships with two banks of oarsmen were called biremes, those with three, triremes. The Greek trireme was a sleek, fast warship. At the front it carried a metal-plated battering ram for crippling enemy ships. In 480 B.C., there was a sea battle at Salamis, between 310 triremes and 800 Persian ships.

Greek trireme about 500 B.C.

Who won the Battle of Salamis?

It was won by the Greeks. They out-maneuvered the Persians and caused havoc by ramming their ships. At the end of the day, the Persians had lost 200 ships and the Greeks only 40.

Did early warships ever use sail-power?

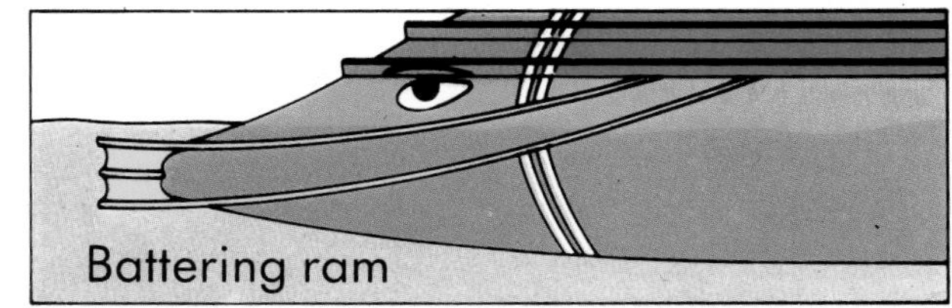

Battering ram

HMS Victory

In 1805, Britain and France were at war. Their rival fleets, of huge three-masted wooden warships carrying up to 100 guns, each tried to gain control of the seas. They met in a decisive battle off Cape Trafalgar, Spain, on October 21. The commander of the British Fleet was Admiral Lord Nelson in his flagship HMS *Victory*. He ordered his ships to break into the enemy line, firing broadside after broadside of iron cannonballs. Eighteen French ships were either destroyed or captured.

What is a broadside?

When all the cannons on one side of a warship are fired at once, this is called a broadside. The gun crews in ships at this time worked in terrible conditions. The gundecks were filled with choking, blinding smoke from the cannons, and the noise was so loud that many sailors were permanently deafened.

What is a flagship?

HMS *Victory*

Gun team

Iron and steam

The invention of steam-powered engines in the mid-1800s made it possible to build heavily armored warships. These were called ironclads, and were driven through the water by propeller. Ironclads first met in battle in 1862, during the American Civil War. The North's *Monitor* and the *Merrimac* of the South blasted at each other for three hours, but neither ship could damage the other.

How many guns did these ships have?

Merrimac had ten guns – four on each side and one at each end. *Monitor* had two guns mounted on a revolving turret. Both ships' guns fired explosive shells instead of cannon balls, but even these could not penetrate the ships' thick iron armor.

What fuel did these ships use?

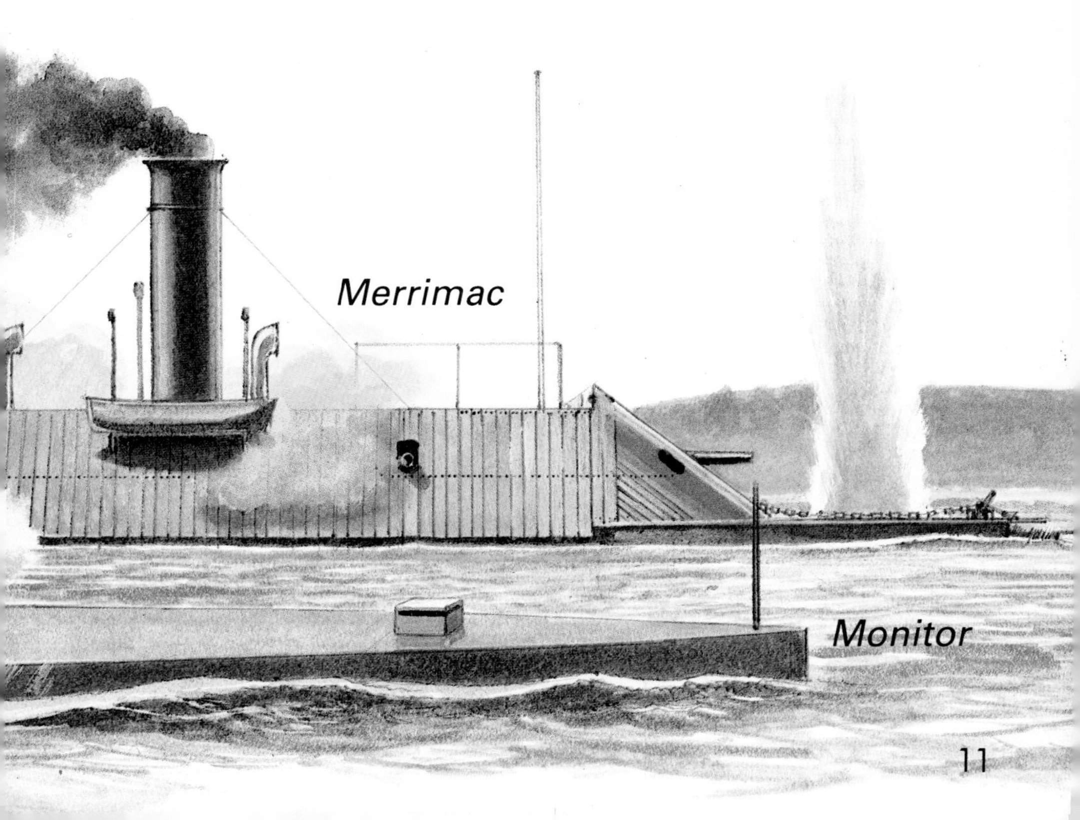

The Dreadnoughts

At the outset of World War I (1914-18), both Britain and Germany had powerful navies. Pride of their fleets were the huge Dreadnought battleships, named after the HMS *Dreadnought*, built in Britain in 1906. Dreadnoughts had ten main guns, all of the same size – 30 cm (12 ins) – mounted on five twin turrets. In addition, they carried over 20 smaller guns. With a top speed of over 22 knots, the Dreadnoughts were the most powerful warships that the world had ever seen.

HMS *Dreadnought*

Did the Dreadnoughts ever meet in battle?

They met only once, in the Battle of Jutland in the North Sea in 1916. There were 151 British ships and 101 German ships. A great many lives were lost and neither side could claim victory. Afterward, neither fleet put to sea again during the course of the war.

How fast is a speed of 22 knots?

Firepower

The main guns of a World War I battleship could hit moving targets at a range of more than 14 km (9 miles). The ammunition was stored well below the deck, in the ship's magazine, to protect it from enemy fire. Shells were hoisted up the ammunition tube to the shell chamber, and then passed to the loading bay, where the gun was loaded by hand. This arrangement also protected the ship's ammunition from the danger of being ignited by a flashback when the gun was fired.

Do today's warships have guns like this?

The main guns on today's warships are automatically loaded and can fire up to 2,000 shells a minute. They are used to defend the ship against enemy aircraft, and to attack land and sea targets. Most modern warships are also armed with powerful missiles.

What is meant by a gun's "range"?

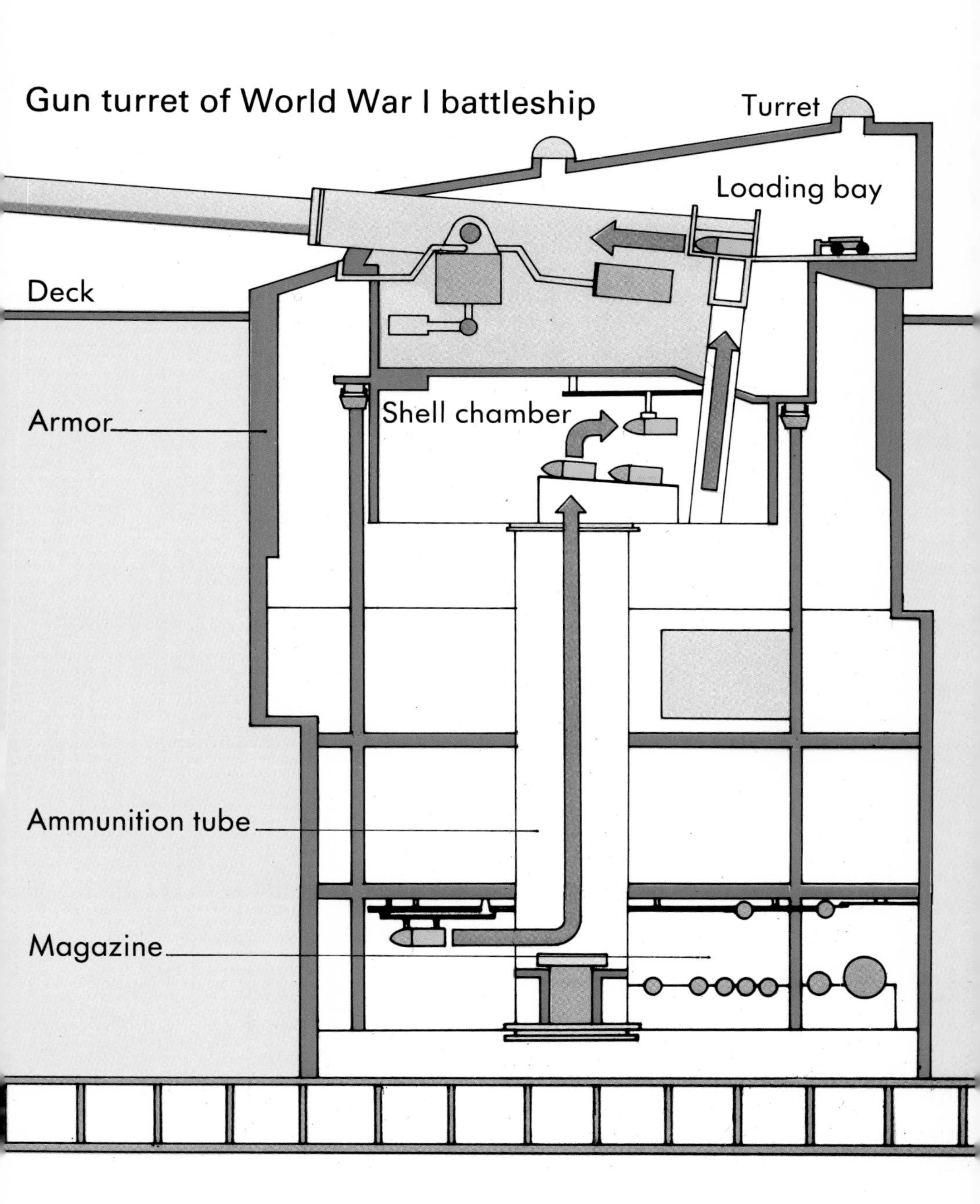
Gun turret of World War I battleship
Turret
Loading bay
Deck
Armor
Shell chamber
Ammunition tube
Magazine

The Graf Spee

The *Admiral Graf Spee*

After World War I, Germany was not allowed to have a strong fleet of heavy battleships. So during the 1930s she built three "pocket battleships" instead. These were the first major warships to be given diesel engines. They were armed with powerful guns, and with a top speed of more than 26 knots they could outpace most other battleships of their day. The most famous of these three ships was the *Admiral Graf Spee*.

Why was the Graf Spee *famous?*

Using a seaplane for spotting, the *Admiral Graf Spee* sank nine merchant ships in the first few weeks of World War II (1939-45). In December 1939, she was engaged by three British cruisers off the coast of South America. The captain fled into a harbor and "scuttled," or sank, the ship himself.

What is a cruiser?

Aircraft carriers

Aircraft carriers are the heart of a modern surface fleet. The American USS *Nimitz* is the largest warship ever built. It has two nuclear reactors to power its engines, and can stay at sea for 13 years without refueling. The *Nimitz* has a crew of over 6,000 and carries more than 100 aircraft.

USS *Nimitz*

How do the planes land and take off?

They are launched by steam catapults. These can propel a jet fighter to over 270 km/h (167 mph) in less than a second. To land, the pilot comes in on full power and catches one of four arrester wires with a hook on the aircraft's tail.

Why does the pilot come in on full power?

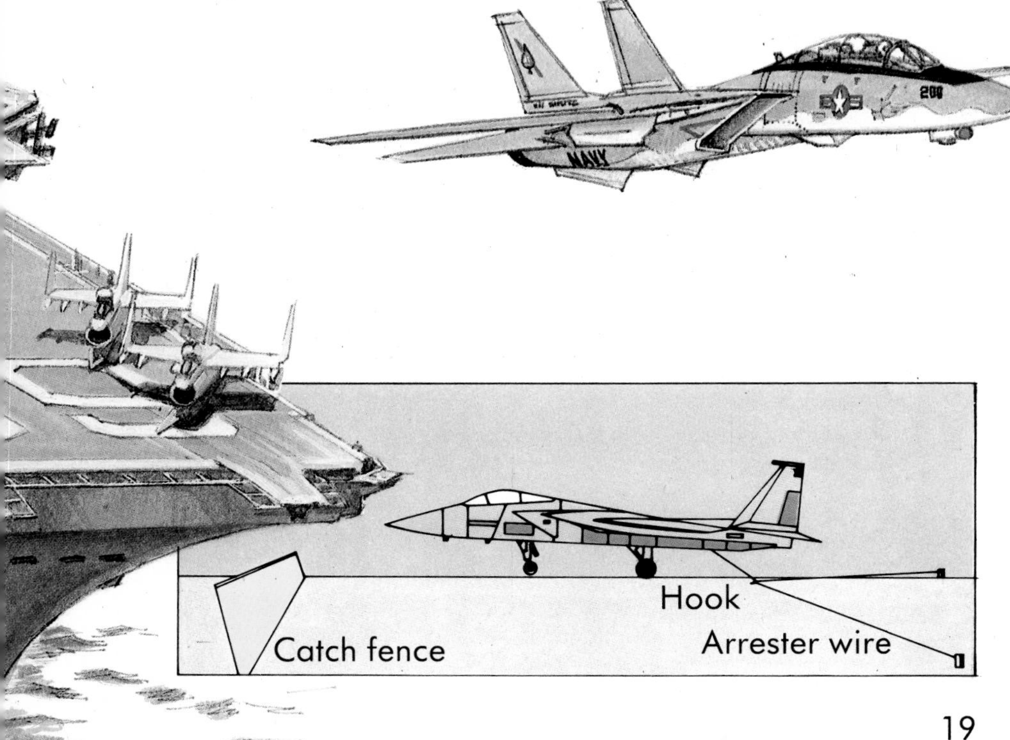

Destroyers

The main job of destroyers and frigates is to protect the fleet from enemy air attack and to seek out and destroy enemy submarines. Destroyers are the larger of the two types, and are armed with guns, missiles, depth charges and anti-submarine torpedoes. Many frigates and destroyers carry helicopters. The large white dome on the destroyer *Suffren*, shown here, houses the ship's radar system.

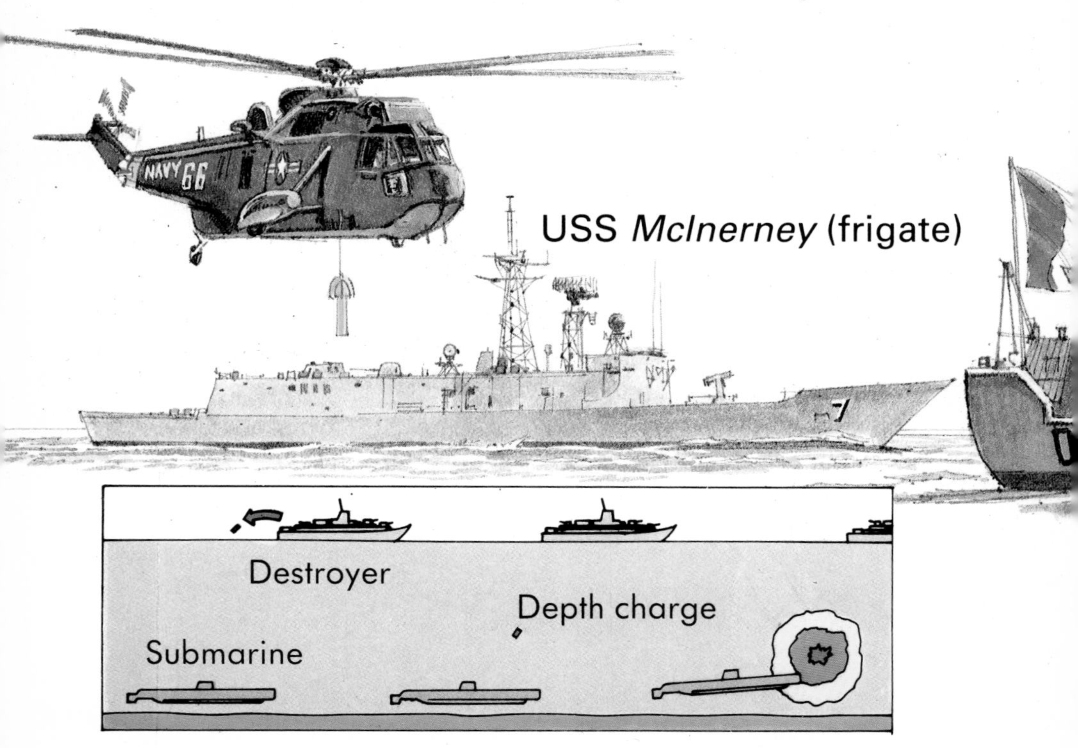

How do destroyers attack submarines?

Submarines are very hard to detect. Helicopters dangle sound detecting equipment in the ocean. When an enemy sub is found, it may be attacked with depth charges, or torpedoes.

What is a depth charge?

Suffren (destroyer)

Modern weapons

Although modern warships still have guns, their most powerful weapons are missiles. Once launched, many missiles seek out their targets using radar. Missiles such as the *Seawolf* are used to defend the ship against enemy missiles. *Seawolf* can hit targets as small as a 15 cm (6 ins) shell traveling at supersonic speed.

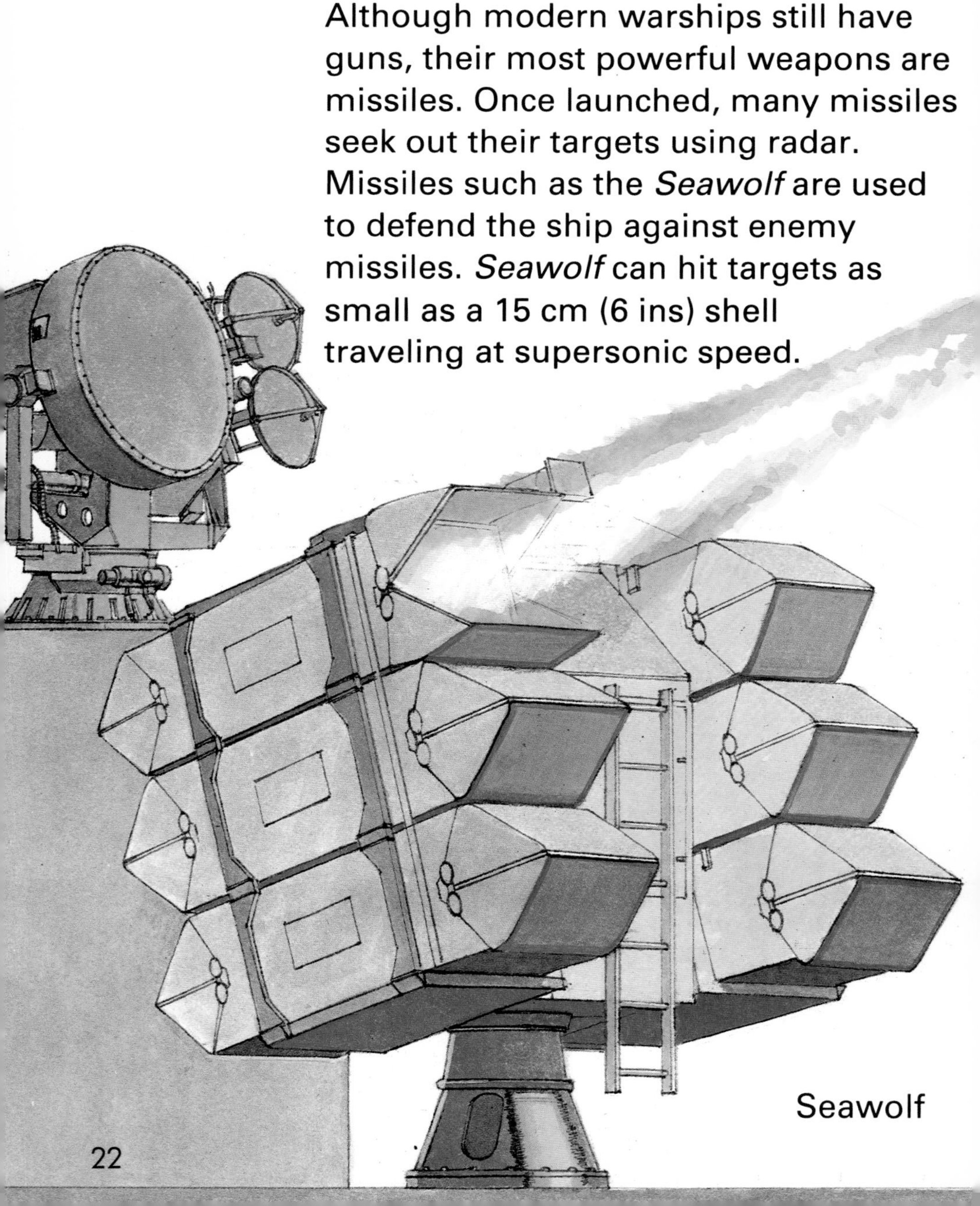

Seawolf

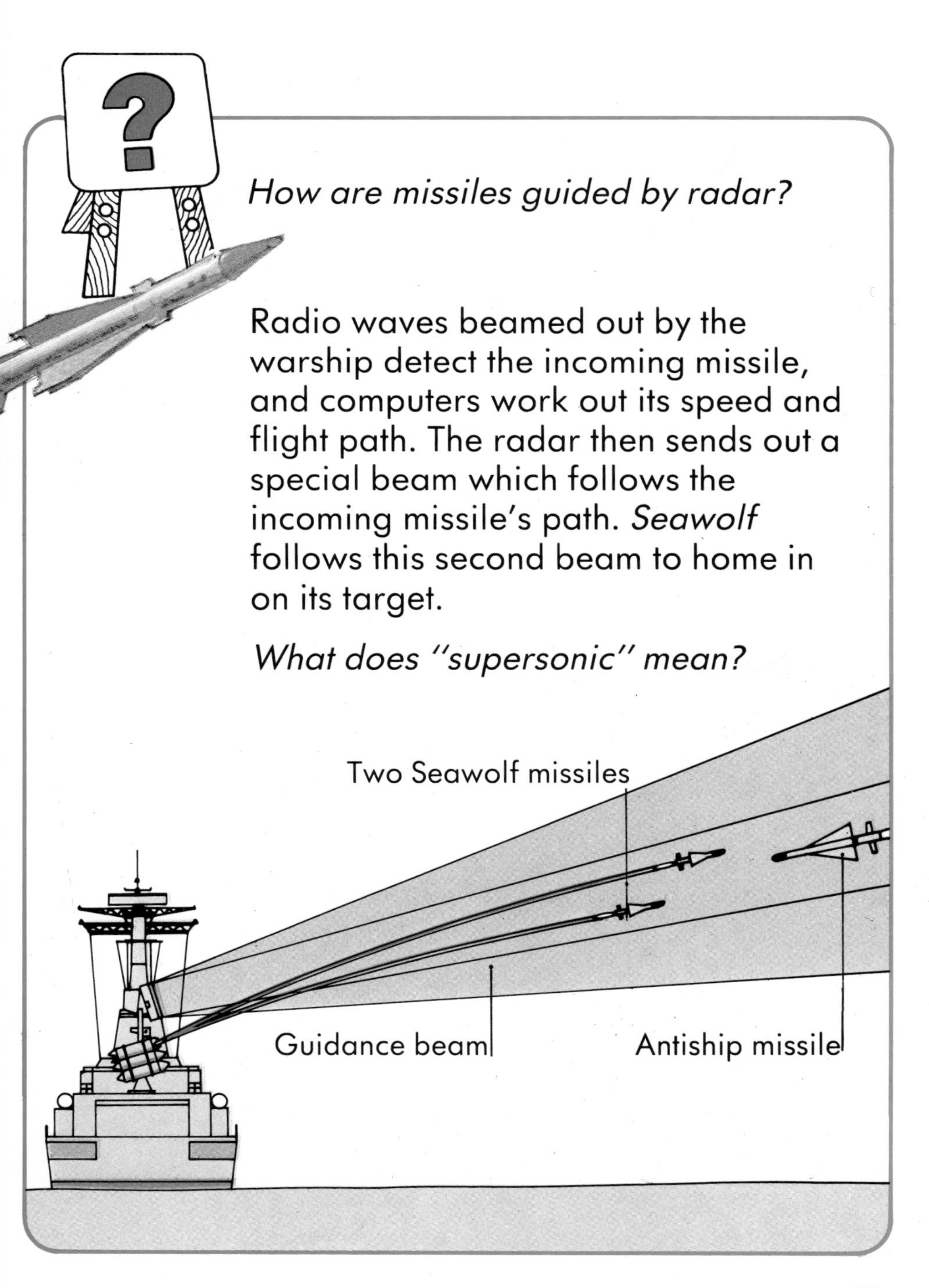

How are missiles guided by radar?

Radio waves beamed out by the warship detect the incoming missile, and computers work out its speed and flight path. The radar then sends out a special beam which follows the incoming missile's path. *Seawolf* follows this second beam to home in on its target.

What does "supersonic" mean?

Minehunters

A mine is an underwater explosive, usually moored by cable at a certain depth, or laid on the seabed. Minehunters are ships designed to detect and destroy them. Modern minehunters are built of non-magnetic reinforced plastic. They carry remote-control minehunters. These use TV cameras and sonar equipment to seek out enemy mines.

Italian *Lerici* minehunter

Why are minehunters non-magnetic?

Many mines are detonated by the magnetic field given out by a ship passing overhead. Others are set off by pressure waves in the ocean, or by the sound waves sent by a ship's engines.

What is sonar?

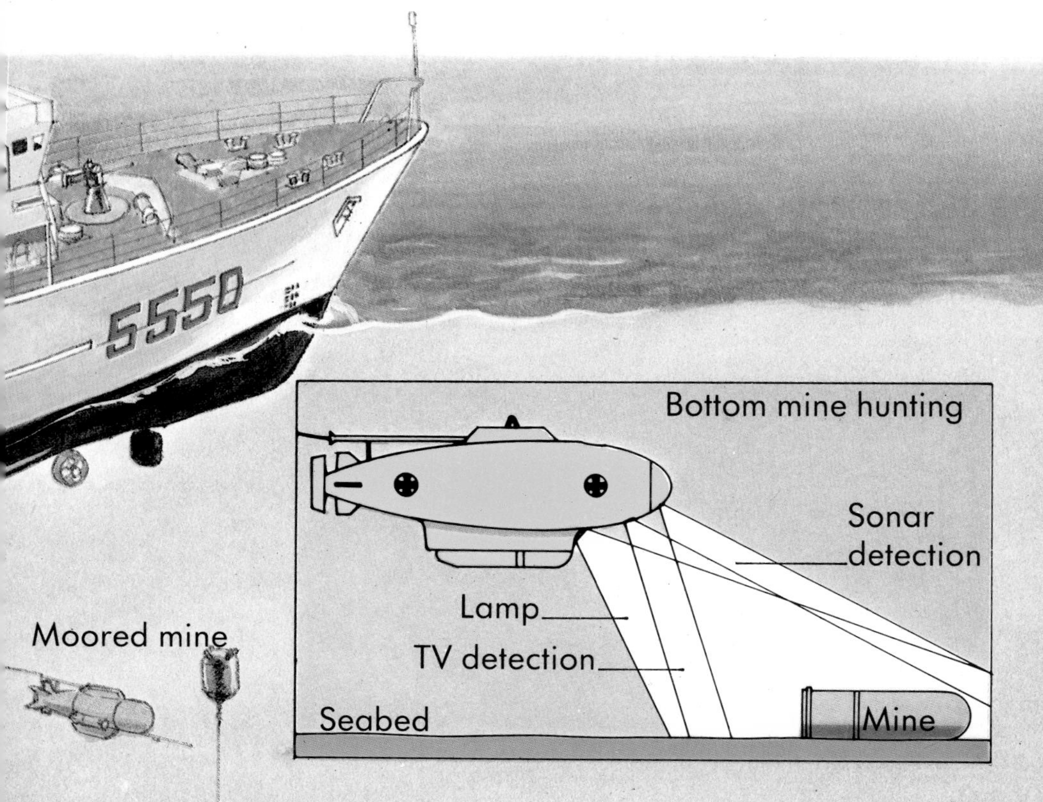

The future

Many experts think that the warships of the future will not be giants like the USS *Nimitz*. Such ships could easily be detected and attacked by submarines and missiles. Instead, future warships will be small, fast, and armed with the latest missiles and laser weapons. Such ships might be raised on hydrofoils, like the one shown below.

What are hydrofoils?

A hydrofoil is a metal plate, or fin, on a ship's hull. As the ship speeds up, water pressure under the hydrofoil lifts the ship out of the water.

What ideas do you have about future warships?

Future hydrofoil warship

Answers

Did early warships ever use sail power?

These early warships used sails while in the open sea, but before they entered battle the sail and mast were lowered.

What is a flagship?

A flagship is the leading ship of the fleet, captained by the fleet's commander.

What fuel did these ships use?

They used coal. This was burned to heat water to produce steam that drove the ships' engines.

How fast is a speed of 22 knots?

Ships' speed is usually measured in knots. A knot is a speed of one nautical mile per hour. A nautical mile measures 1,852 m (6,076 ft).

What is meant by a gun's "range"?

It means the furthest distance that a gun can fire its shell.

What is a cruiser?

A cruiser is a warship that is smaller than a battleship, has thinner armor and less powerful guns.

Why does the pilot come in on full power?

If his plane fails to catch an arrester wire when he lands, he must have sufficient power to be able to take off again for a second landing attempt.

What is a depth charge?

A depth charge is an explosive device, set to explode at a certain depth.

What does "supersonic" mean?

Supersonic means faster than the speed of sound. At sea level this is 1,226 km/h (760 mph).

What is sonar?

Sonar stands for *S*ound *N*avigation *R*anging. Active sonar systems send out sound waves and pick up their reflection when they hit an object in the ocean. Passive sonar simply picks up all the sounds of the sea.

Index